RICHARD HILL

UAW UNION

From my Perspective

Contents

Preface

This is a book about the changes that I have experienced, how the workforce and management have changed during my employment at Saginaw Steering Gear.

Chapter 1

Graduation:

I graduated Arthur Hill High School in 1972 a class of over 750 students in Saginaw, Michigan. As I explained in the introduction, my family on the Hill side started and worked in the auto industry for General Motors. My dad (Norman C. Hill) worked at Hill's Tavern. The business was owned back then, was my Great Grandma (Della Pearl,Hill) and Uncle (Lee Hill.) My dad worked the day shift 9 am-5pm and my uncle lee worked 5 pm- till closing.

My dad said to me; early on about my junior year in high school said I need not worry about my grades because he could not afford college tuition for me. Why am I telling you this because I am trying to give you the mind set of the generations in that time frame, 1971 going forward.

The Vietnam war or conflict was going on then but was starting to wind down in troop strength. So I was looking at two options not three. Meaning most students my age and with similar skill- set could either join the Armed forces, go to a University or try to get employment at one of the seven auto plants in the Saginaw,MI area at that time. My dad talked me out of joining the Army because he said it was to political of a War/Conflict.

I did not think much about where or what I would do for a job where you can make decent money to live on. I was thinking of going on vacation after I graduated high school. I did construction work every summer since I was 14 years old. After graduation I went to California with my best friend the Summer after I received my High School Diploma. We stayed in California for a two weeks and then flew to Las Vegas to see Elvis Presley at the Hilton International, which has changed ownership and renamed Westgate Las Vegas Resort and Casino. I was eighteen years old, and saw the King of Rock and Roll do the best live show ever.

Chapter 2

The Dream:

After Summer of 1972 I had put in an application at Saginaw Steering Gear. I got a call to take a physical to see if I was healthy enough to work at the hourly jobs. I had passed all their requirements and just waited for a call when they would be hiring off the street again. I got a call to interview with a manager up at plant three which was the World Head Quarters. I went in and answered some question from my personal interview and he just said come back after I got a hair cut. I did that the same day and went back to see him. I was given an employment opportunity at plant seven on October 3, 1972.

Everyone that hired into the plant had a 90 day trail period which they could fire you on the spot for cause or no cause. My dad said never turn down overtime for the first 90 days because they would fire the ones who didn't work it within their first 90 days. This is before before you could be a card carrying Union member at Local 699 Saginaw, MI. After a year you had almost all the current benefits, one was job security.

When I was being introduced to my Foreman he did not have a thumb on his right hand. Then I met the job setter he was the guy who knew how to fix and adjust the production machines in the department. He did not have a thumb on his right hand. I was starting to get a little concerned about that fact and I did not ask them how their injury happened.

After working at GM for over a year a worker could go to College while working at the plant. If you got a passing grade the company would reimburse you for your class and they had at the time a $100 dollar allowance for your class books. I was bored with the daily monotony of my job and I was getting letters from Delta to apply to their school and pick a better job. I threw them away, but one day I read the letter and decided to call them. I first met with a guidance consular to figure out my new career path. Skill Trades, or engineering is about it for my list. I was accepted and started out registering for the mandatory classes that everyone had to take. I started out with going into the engineering field, later I would change my mind, but you have to start somewhere.

As for the benefits after your 90 days you are now qualified for medical benefits, pension,vacation time off. As time went on we negotiated for dental benefits and could get reimbursed for your kids college education. The amount was a sum allotted once per year. It did not cover everything, but it sure did help. We got national holidays paid time off. We did have personal paid holidays about nine of them, but then they where negotiated back. Profit sharing came in to play later in the eighties. Maternity time off paid for six weeks, it is eight weeks now. Paid Paternity leave two weeks now, they did not have it when I worked there. They had 4 weeks of unpaid family leave when I was working. They now have twelve weeks paid leave for taking care of a parent with serious health issues and for parents to bond with their new child or to care for a spouse with a health issue. This is in addition to the paid maternity leave. There is no pension for the new lower tier employees.

Chapter 3

The way out and Crazy:

In the 70's a lot of guys around my age at the time would work for a year and then quit and go onto something else. I would never see them again and some I knew from High School and from the old neighborhood. One time after working at (SSG) for a year, while I was walking down the isle I heard screaming and at a loud voice shouting. I went down there to see what was going on and a guy a little older then me lost it and could not understand everyone just working at the same type of job on the assemble line day in and day out. He was lead by management to the medical office at plant seven. I found out later he quit and ended up buying and running a popular steak house in Saginaw. Others later where going out on medical issues with their mental state. I did not understand the problem and yet some guys bragged about it. I guess they wanted to get work-comp money or medical leave and then doing work on the outside construction, contracting work or whatever to double their monetary income. Some people felt like doing an honest days work for an honest weeks pay. I however was not sure about my future at (SSG) I had just had an injury to my left index finger at work. After healing up, I was determined not to quit and make the best of it until I had an education and skills to increase my prospects.

When you first hire in your seniority starts that day. Which means from that hire date everyone hired in before you has more time and everyone hired in after you has less seniority. You have more seniority time to bump to a new shift or get a better job because of how much time you have. If nobody has paperwork in for a job and the position becomes open then management has the right to put whomever they want into that position. The two positions open when you first hire into the plant, is that you are either assigned to the assemble line or you go to a production department. There was more overtime in the production departments, because they had to make the parts from different production departments to put the product together on the assemble line. We made steering gears, steering columns and much more.

As for school I ended up getting accepted at Delta College and getting my grade point up to 3.5 at Delta College over the years and decided to apply to Western Michigan University to finish my associates degree.

After getting there I found out I was not mature enough to focus on my studies. There was a party every night somewhere. To much living life opportunities and experiences, where there was a lot of education, but not in the books. That is another story for anther book or time.

Fast forward to 1980 to 1983, we were coming out of one of the highest inflationary time so people were not buying cars. Thus began the layoffs, I was not affected, but many were and some never were called back to work. After about 1984 the economy was starting to pick back up and the race was on to fill the demand for auto parts for cars and trucks. Ronald Reagan the 40th President got us back working again. Six days a week on the assembly lines and seven days a week with plenty of overtime during the week in the production departments.

Chapter 4

Getting involved in the Politics:

The UAW before I came to work at SSG was established by the first progressive President of the UAW a man by the name of Walter Reuther. He was killed in a plan crash in 1970, but was instrumental with organizing at the Detroit plants and the sit down strike in Flint, Michigan. He was the main visionary of the Black Lake facility in Onaway, MI. The Black Lake facility has created a magnificent opportunity for the membership to be trained and educated on the UAW history, current laws, learning about the legislative elected leaders that support our cause. The buildings at Black Lake have areas where members can exchange ideas and listen to other members concerns to grow the membership. To learn and hear from other union people from different States, different unions and the problems they have and brain storm ideas for our wants and needs for our union as a whole.

Leonard F. Woodcock was elected to the Presidency of the UAW after Walters death. He was one of the members that fought along side of Walter in the early days when the UAW was finding itself. Back before I had my 90 days in the plant the

UAW called for a strike in 1972. I was working in a production department and was being overseen by my junior foreman when the word came down and a committee man named Bob Bacon came around his district which I was in and yelled to everyone to shut the machines off. I looked at my foreman and he just shrugged his shoulders and I followed the order. This went for all members and non union card carrying members. Bob was one of the last of the old school hard-line union members. They knew the sacrifices the people went through to get the negotiated benefits to where currently and what necessities the UAW member needed to negotiate in future contracts with the Big three. Looking back it was a proud moment back when a mans man was your committeeman. Not like the the ones elected after guys like Bob left office I am not sure what became of Bob, but I wish him and his family the best. The committee persons that people elected after the 70's going forward into the 80's were opportunist, not all but most of them. They would rather give back what gains we made in the contracts then fight for our bigger piece of the pie. Most of the time people who ran for office to become the next committeeman. Would go soft and take the bribes that management gave to them in return for not enforcing the rules to make conditions better for the worker. Management knew they had a formula to convince whom ever ran and won the office of union rep. They would fail our memberships expectations. If they did a good enough job they would make the union rep a manager, foreman etc. They would leave the union ranks and be on managements payroll. The rest of them would stay in an hourly position, but management would transfer them out of the area into another plant because of a possible retaliation against them by the membership.

There where eight separate plants in the SSG complex. I was currently working at plant six for the 80's decade. I would complain about the committee persons work ethic about representing the rules for us union members in our department. This went on for awhile and finally a member asked me if I thought that the rep would change his ways. I said no, so he said if I wanted change then I better run for office. I thought about it and decided that some one had to put their money where their mouth was so I committed to run for the position the next time the election came to make that change.

I lost my first try at the job by 2 votes. I was totally confused because according to the general consensuses of my district which consisted of 3 to 5 departments depending on the number of people in them. I was a lock for the election to get voted in. I found out fifteen years later by one of the chairpersons of the election committee that she had fixed the hand count because she loved Gary Shepherd which was the skilled trades committee man. I was not sure what was the issue with Gary had about me then, but I am sure whatever he was concerned about or afraid of eased his mind, but it took away from the union membership who expressed their will, with whom they wanted to represent them. Gary went on to the Region 1D rep position and gets a pension from the Union also, as well as a GM one. Fixing an election is a federal crime. He is not a real union brother in the spirit of the Ideology. This is just one example of what came after the 70's. They are only looking out for what they can get for themselves and pretending to be looking out for the membership.

I went on to transfer to plant three in the 1990's and worked on the assembly line again. From there after about 6 months I transferred up to the front office area as a custodial engineer. I went to the union meetings once a month on Sunday. I was a Democrat at the time. I was elected to the election committee by the membership for one term. I was appointed to the consumers affairs rep for 9 years under two different Caucasus. Normally when one side wins the majority they clean house, but I was asked to stay on, because I did a great job, they told me. I filled in as committee man for my District for many years for John Polzin. He was one of our last chances to turn things around before the bankruptcy.

Chapter 5

Job Security:

As the eighties passed as a whole the auto industry was going through changes. The foreign auto companies wanted to keep selling there products in the USA without the large tariffs put on their products. The congress made a law that to escape paying higher tariffs on their products 50% of their car parts had to made in the USA. Thus the building of factories by the foreign car companies began. The American made car companies began to spin off parts of the business, close some plants and consolidate the factories to meet the lesser demand.

Closing various assembly plants and making other plants making similar products start adding more shifts to work around the clock at the plants management kept open for production. This meant that some States would lose tax dollars and the ones that stayed open made concessions to keep them open. Like tax abatement, more favorable rules that favored management at the workers expense.

Marching into the 1990's as a worker with enough seniority to keep from getting laid off was temporary security for me and members with similar seniority. The new strategy for General

Motors was to spin off most of the parts plants and make them a new company called Delphi, which would be separate from GM. They would have their own stock listed on the stock market also.

The effects on the union workers from their plant closing was painful enough. The union negotiated job transfers with a set amount of money to be given to the employees to move or drive to the new job site for them. The amount was based then by the amount of miles you had to transfer to your new destination. Also there was a term called the jobs bank for employees that were either laid off due to little work or the department they worked in was sold or transferred to to another plant. They would have the right to transfer with the job or stay home and wait for a job opportunity to open up in another plant or the one they were laid off from. Some would not go anywhere and stayed home an collected a 40 hour check every week. This was the unions answer to increase the cost of moving or closing a factory. When a major assembly plant closed with over 20,000 thousand employees. Like in Michigan it would create major stress on families because the husband, wife or maybe both would lose their job without enough seniority to retire. So they would have to put in for a choice of a new plant in another state sometime and the lucky ones got a job transfer closer to home. The people effected by the transfer would sometimes not want to leave the area, because the Grandparents, mom and dad, extended family in the area. The wife or the husband might have to leave to keep the job with the benefits in tack. So one would leave for the job and work there until they had enough time to retire and drive or fly back home on occasion. This worked for some, but the majority of the time it did not. So the divorce lawyers made bank at the union workers expense. If the employee was offered a transfer they had three opportunities to take the transfer, if after the third option to go was refused the employees seniority would freeze and their benefits like health care would discontinue. They would have an option to buy Cobra insurance if they could afford it.

Point of information: The contract between Management and the UAW was negotiated as the shrinking of the automobile plants progressed. This might be in between the four year contract. So it was ad hoc as the downsizing proceeded.

Chapter 6

The Meaning of Solidarity:

Definition: Unity or agreement of feeling or action, especially among individuals with a common interest mutual support within a group. Ex:"Factory worker voiced solidarity with the striking students."

That was true of some but not all. Example: Unanimity; The state or quality of being unanimous; a consensus or undivided opinion. That would be true at the UAW National Convention, but if there was Opposition from a local union chapter being represented by their trustees to the convention. The power at Solidarity house would have that factory negotiated closed and the production of products produced there would be farmed out to various other plants.

One practice by a union member which was finally put to rest was when a union worker would put in a suggestion for an award of 10,000 to 20,000 dollars. The suggestion would be to eliminate a job on the assembly line or production job. However the work would be increased to other employees. This would at times be less safe for the employee and would cause more health issues and injuries, the most common was carpal tunnel syndrome. This practice of eliminating another union job by a brother or sister of the union was eventually stopped by a grass roots movement where a person to make any suggestion to eliminate a job would be kicked out of the union and back then you could not work in a closed shop if you were not a union member in good standing. It is a fact of life here in the USA, if there is no recourse, penalty for a certain behavior most people of low morale or ethics would keep getting richer off the fellow union members back. Also as time went on from the 1980's to the end of 2003. I saw and heard that members in certain departments like skilled trades, prototype department, tool and die grinder dept, allowed the Union reps at the time to negotiate away the work of these departments to other facilities the GM Corporation was building and hiring non-union workers at with a lower cost for hourly pay. How did this happen you wonder, I was amazed that the workers in those departments were allowed to work and get paid twelve hours a day seven days a week and did little work. Some did not even have to show up to work. So what legacy is that for looking out for the people and membership. Thus the people coming to work in these departments behind them would not have an opportunity or job that they had to go to school for to be able to apply for them. They did not know and would not understand why their senior brothers and sisters would do such a thing. This was the part where I knew we were in trouble big time. The cost not only to the membership, but to all the stake holders in the area that would supply the membership and the employees at SSG with their wants and needs. Saginaw, MI is barely a shadow of it's once thriving and growing City. People have to go were the work is. The remaining leadership at Solidarity House says that the membership is all one. They say that with a straight face while there is and has been a two tier membership since 2008 to the present 2023.

Chapter 7

Rule changes from 1972 to 1989 in the National and Local contracts:

First I want to recognize the workers at the Ford company that in 1937 asked for bread and got bullets instead. Four were killed and 60 were wounded. This is what I mean when I say the old school, the pain and sacrifice these people made so the working conditions and benefits for the worker of my time, before and after was a lot more bearable. The union reps from the 1980's onward mostly wanted to give up our rights and benefits to keep our jobs, they believed by acquiescing to Managements demands they would leave us along. This is one of the reasons why there needed to be more education for all the employees on the UAW history and the union Ideology. But as we know management just keep taking until you are not a union anymore and reward the carpet beggars. The company would rather have the power to work you as long as hard as they can until you get hurt, can't work the job anymore for health reasons or are killed. They do not want to recognize you as a human being, you are just another cog in the wheel. They will just hire an younger employee and do the same to them.

Back in 1972 after I hired into Saginaw Steering Gear to work and belong to the union, which was your life line to a livable middle class life. I did not understand how much the right to your job was and protected by the UAW until I watched five union reps walk a person down the front isle to the assembly line to give him his job back. I asked who the person was and what was going on. The reply I got was that this man had spent some years in jail for a crime, I am not sure of, but the word was that he got caught dealing drugs. This was what the belief was back then and how a generation felt about it. I am not sure when the right to your union job was negotiated away, but like anything some people abuse what was a good thing and make it not so. I think in the eighties after the just say no program by then 1st Lady Nancy Reagan, if you where caught dealing drugs you could be fired. To elaborate on the guaranteed job program, it worked for its intended purpose in the years prior to me hiring in to SSG per my understanding. You could get your job back after being convicted of a crime, gone to jail for over five years, I am not positive on the contractual language on that. You would not earn seniority while incarcerated. You would get your benefits back once you started working again and the clock on your pension would start again.

The Vietnam conflict was happening from 1965 to 1975 the years when the President declared it a war or conflict. Men where drafted then and some did join for patriotic reasons. If you were working for GM and after you got your 1 year in the plant and USA service drafted you, GM would release you and you would still receive you seniority time to go towards your pension. If you were lucky enough to survive your time in the US service you would be back working at GM. I do not remember meeting anyone working that had a physical injury at least one I could see from locking at them and working with them. I worked on the assemble line then at plant six and a few times I worked with guys that were less then three days to three weeks from being Honorably discharged. Let me tell you, they told me stories about their experiences over in Vietnam that I will not repeat out of respect for these guys. Most of them knew as I would tell them that all my uncles served in the Korean conflict in all branches, Army, Navy, Air force. I loved to talk with them and just listen to their stories, what a better way to make time fly on the line. Later I would realize that they told me stories that they could not even tell their wife. Remember we started getting cable and they did not cover the (PTS) **"Post-traumatic Stress"** problems the men had coming back home from Country(Vietnam). Post Traumatic Stress Disorder as an example: I was working with a gentleman I can not remember his name but I do remember his face. We worked on the line and in Heat Treat department; that is where the big gas furnaces where. WE had a cooling machine where we could keep our pop's or sodas cold. This was great in the Summer time. I cant' really remember him telling me any Vietnam stories. He keep ever thing inside I guess, but he seemed like a nice guy. I think he was back in the USA less then a year and he eventually killed his wife and kid or kids. People did not talk much about things like that then. There was one Vietnam Vet of which word went around the line that he was not all there in the head. He came to work every day and did his job. If you had to work overtime together sorting parts you just kept to yourself because some thing you might say would set him off. He tried to kill a foreman I was told, he chased him around the assemble line, lucky for the foreman he did not get caught by him.

The worker has to work with the rules that management

puts out. They only care about a body that causes no trouble and comes to work, every day but we have to be aware of the issues of our work environment, now they have Hipaa rules. Some of the guys that talked with me about their experience while serving Vietnam while we worked on the line side by side. After we got to learn about one another we began a friendship, a mutual respect for one another. Once I understood the stories were true they were never brought up again. I held them in confidence because they were not a danger to themselves or other people, unless you messed with them. One more story to add, there was another Vietnam Vet working in Heat treat dept where I was at the time. Two guys that I got along with not much older the me, 19 to 24 I would guess came up to me laughing their buts off. I asked them what was so funny, while I was working my machine. They asked me to take a break and they will show me. I walked back to the heat treat area to an place which had giant furnaces and there was a small footprint job where a man was working with his back to us. He was new and just back from country . He had dark glasses on because he had been hurt by a hand grenade.

The guys lifted a quarter size cardboard pallet and then dropped it on the cement floor. It made a big bang sound and the guy on the machine just hit the ground faster then I had ever seen. I was so mad at them the two guys I went from 0 to 60 in a sec I was so mad I did not understand how any one would treat our armed service men like that. They both ran because I was yelling at them and would have hit them, I was pissed that they would do that to one of our guys. It was different times back them when a lot of people were against the war. I never spoke to those two guys again.

Fast forward to 1985, after the plant closings and consolidations, people stated to move and transfer to other plants that had openings. This caused some problems with seniority which affected who got the job or any position up for grabs first choice and with shift preference. Example: some person from another plant transfers in to your department and you have been waiting for a job that is high in demand and the person takes the spot because they have more seniority then you and is only at your plant because of a plant closure. So the UAW negotiated with GM, Ford and Chrysler to implement a 1/7/1985 seniority date when you get transferred to another facility. That means that if you have 1/7/81 and the other person has a 1/7/1972. They have to go with the 1/7/1985 date when transferring. This means you have more time if you hired into the plant before 1/07/1985, you have more seniority then they do for a shift or job preference. If two people transfer into the department and they both have 1/7/1985 after that date they will go buy their original hire in date to get the job position or shift preference. Business and the economy was growing so there were not many plant closings to take us past 1989.

Chapter 8

Elections and the hidden benefits:

To run for a district committee person, shop person; this position covers the entire plant up to so many people. If there are more people in a plant then negotiated for the Shop man to handle, on the floor they will redistrict the shop map and elect another shop position to handle the number of people. That was true at plant 6 which had two shop positions. As you get more familiar with the system you may want to run for bargaining Chairman or Local Union President. There are the Trustee positions, Guide, Sargent at arms,Treasure and many more. You can look them up per union contract at a factory. Every position has it's up and down side.

One reason reason people want to run to be a committee person is the overtime, some do it for the membership, but not many as there should be and I blame that on our education of the membership. On the functioning as committee man per overtime, there has to be some one that fills in as committee man if so many people work either 4 to eight hours a day overtime or overtime on the week ends. What triggers this is that some departments work and others do not because of the need for there particular type of part/product. If out of that x amount of union workers working overtime have to be represented by a committee person. This goes for the first, second and third shifts. This is the same for the Shop steward position because they have to responsible for every one in the plant. In the 1990's you could go on certain types of meetings, between management and the union leadership and get paid from the plant/GM/Delphi. The more time you go on union training, outings,business, etc. You will get your lost time at the plant and the local union will pay you with union funds from dues paid every month. I would be invited to go to Black Lake for training and education. I would meet people from different unions and States. Some times after the meetings and dinner, oh yes you eat very well at Black Lake. Some of the union reps would complain about their local issues and they looked like they had a lot of sonority at least more then me and a long time at their position, I think to long. I would be curious and ask why have the problems at their factory been going on for so long and have you not taken back the ideas from our training at class. They would say to me and everyone who would listen that no one wants to get involved or cares about the issues or to come up to Black Lake for training. I did not say anything back because, I have found while working at the plant that if you correct the person with logic or common since. They will end up hating you and tell every one that you are a low down dirty dog. Some time idiots like that have a powerful friend up the ladder in the union. Thus the guy was from the Pittsburgh, PA I thought I could not change anything from my post because he was drinking before, during and after the discussion. This is another example of stagnation of learned knowledge to the good old boy cronyism. This is one of many reasons the union Ideology of sacrifice for the good of the whole, it was like they had the position and felt entitled even at the workers demise. Thus the morale goes down with the membership, because they are not getting the answers to their issues or current news relaid to the membership at the focal point of Black Lake training. Why you ask, well sometimes the people sent to go to the training and get paid to go to classes, they end up partying and not going to the classes or doing their job. What they are paid by union funds to do. The Union Ideology just dissipated and made way for the opportunist that milk the system dry until it finally breaks. In my opinion the current membership today should start a movement to change their structure to a more international program such as the World Socialist Party Of the Fourth International (WSWS). These are Trotskyist which are following the teachings of Leon Trotsky.

The game has changed and there are factories around the world in different foreign Countries. All the workers working in these auto plants need to be united as one to have the leverage to negotiate a livable wage with great benefits. Thus management can't send work over seas and threaten to close more plants in the USA.

Chapter 9

The End Of The Begging:

The 1990's is where the Delphi **spin off** from GM began, which management called it.

Thus if a Delphi plant/factory was scheduled to downsize or close down. If you where affected you had the right to either transfer to another Delphi plant in your area or afar. This did not happen to much as far as I am aware of. You also would have the right to flow back to a GM plant and you would have priority over any one that lost their job at a GM Plant. If you stayed at a Delphi plant your pension and medical benefits would be under the Delphi Flag and in a bankruptcy you could not be covered under the GM umbrella. Delphi even had their own stock which we were encouraged to buy.

After the dust settled from the plant closing and consolidation era, we were coming into the employee buy-out era. This started about 2002 and then there was a tech stock meltdown in the market and the recession was starting for the auto industry around that time frame. I accepted a job transfer back to a GM plant, the first opening was Reno,NV so I took the transfer in 2003

Then in around 2008 there was the near bankruptcy of GM, Chrysler. Ford said that they world sell all of there factories before they world go bankrupt. The big three ask the Union to help and the UAW negotiated a two-tier pay and benefits package for new hires. The union did this in good faith saying this would be only temporary for the new hires and when the economy got back on it feet they would be made whole again with the same pay scale and benefits for all union members. Now 15 years later GM, Ford and Chrysler are making billions and moving into the electric vehicle market. They still have the two tier system and the UAW is silent on this fact. **WE** meaning all the retirees should have cost of living on our pensions also. The present day UAW leadership have lost their purpose and direction. There needs to be a big change in the representation of the current Auto worker. Because Solidarity house bargaining and the leadership are all opportunists where the general consensus of only looking out for one's self or a particular group of people. *While putting the needs and wants of the workers on the jobs in the factory as a minutiae matter.* The leadership tells the current workers that their contract is the best that they can do for them and that they better vote it in or they might close their particular plant or division, or worse.

It is at the point where the current worker does not trust anyone and is told what they have to do to keep their job by both the Management and the UAW. One option to break this yoke of oppression, I found was the (WSWS) The World Socialist Web Site. This could be a great alternative to the current UAW leadership situation and corruption. The UAW started out with Walter, Victor and Ron Reuther at the helm of leading and fighting for better working conditions, medical benefits, pension and paid vacation time off. The Idea was to unite the worker and work together to form a body to form and vote in a Union to fight, negotiate as one to make this demands materialize. The philosophy was a little of a Marxist Idea and how to better serve the auto worker in this case where every worker like Communism, Socialism is paid the same wage, gets better benefits, job security, safer work environment and conditions.

One issue that the current and past leadership did not do was to educate the membership the worker/membership on the purpose of their union it's Ideology. By not implementing this program over the years the leadership turned into a power grab with keeping the membership in the dark about their future. From the late 1980's on up the leadership at all levels but not all, mostly keep the workers on the floor in the dark. Thus these carpetbaggers could keep their bribes and get better perks from GM for doing so.

I felt in 1972 the UAW was strong and powerful. But today 2023 after the plant closings and givebacks, plus the never ending two tier program. The UAW is but an empty shell of what it once was. To change this problem the current auto workforce, needs the help of the upper-tier members, which see what is going on is wrong. They will need the support of the UAW retirees, the ones that understand that our pensions are negotiated not guaranteed. There are over 600,000 thousand UAW retirees. Plus the help of the (WSWS) 4th generation to make this happen. There is a gentleman running for the position of UAW president " Will Lehman" which I have watched the debate on a zoom call between him and four other union members running for that position. Only Will has the workers interest at mind and to fight and negotiate for. He can not do this on his own.

It is a travesty the way the leaders of the UAW says it is with the worker on the floor yet still votes themselves raises at Solidarity House. They also have an extra pension from the UAW treasury with extra health care paid by membership monthly dues. The lower tier has no pension, minimal benefits,job speed ups, poor shop rules, mandatory overtime. You do not have the right to turn it down and if you leave you can be written up or fired.

Chapter 10

Job transfers and the buy-out:

Back in 2003 I got my first opportunity to transfer to UAW Local 1262 Reno, NV. I got there in March of 2003 and worked there until September of 2004. Why so sort of time there, well because they were downsizing from a facility that 800 hundred employees working there to 125 employees at the new Stead, NV template. Now I was low seniority with 1/07/1985 seniority because of my transfer in so I got three chances to take a job transfer and there was no job-bank: waiting at Reno. Where you would get a 40 hr pay check until an opening for an employee on lay-off, could get hired back to the plant to work again. I put in several transfers one at the assembly plant in Arlington, TX . This came up first so I took it. Not knowing anyone there or what the work opportunities were, but I jumped in anyway, I didn't know about any other plant, which was better or worse to work at, so I just took the first offer. Arlington, TX Local 276 is an assembly plant, they put together Escalades, Tahoe, Yukon, and Suburbans.

I had finished my BBA in 2004 at Northwood University so I was trying to get ready for a change. In 2006 being a Team

Leader in Moist Sand Dept. It is where they have eight to ten people in the department. They have sanding stations at various foot prints that sand the imperfections off of the vehicle, before they go to get painted. I was hurt on the line in February of 2006. Later that same year they were coming out with a new buy-out program. This was for people with high seniority like me, and less seniority could retire and still get their pension and benefits. This was open to anyone with various years seniority so they would have a different package per their accumulated seniority. The minimum was ten years I do believe. If you had over 30 yrs the buy-outs would range anywhere from $25,000 to 125,000 plus you still got your pension per your seniority and health care.

Now most of the people left are on the bottom tier with no pension, limited health care and watered down vacation time and 50% vs 100% for tuition assistance now.

Conclusion

Summary and Future:

As mentioned in previous chapters the state of the UAW is in great pearl and has too many rats in there to change themselves. The greed, self righteous, self serving self deceiving leadership offers the workers at the bottom tier no guarantee for a safe and reliable future them and their families. They only look down on that tier as peons, thus if their health goes per injury or illness they are fired and discarded as being of no value. Then they hire younger heather people until their health goes. There is a big fight for change coming and they must win to seek better and more secure representation. This must happen from the ground up. Once the support in numbers materializes, if this does not happen soon nothing will change. For their plate the auto workers need to a organize with workers around the world, because the auto business has changed. GM, Ford, Chrysler, etc. have factories in country's around the world. The workers need to unite together to prevent management from threatening to take work from your plant and move it over seas. If harm is done to one it is done to all. The UAW leadership does not understand this or wants to because, it will take away their power and perks. I pray this will waken auto workers up to fight the worthwhile mission and prepare for the struggles which lay ahead. If they are not successful at changing their leadership and forming a new union for bargaining, there will be little hope for the unskilled factory worker or shilled to improve their current demise and a chance to live a middle class life. They need to control their own destiny and that of the retiree or all will be lost in the end.

Remember: "What can be won at the bargaining table can be lost at the ballot box."

Walter Reuther

Afterword

All is not lost yet. There is still time with effort with perseverance to turn the current condition back to where the body of the whole is one. Because if one of us is hurt, we all are.

Current note the UAW lead by president Shawn Fain are finally getting with United States democratic senators to get them to legislate laws to help get the UAW workers equal pay with benefits. The key is that the Auto industry takes government money for bailouts and contracts. I am very hopeful the leadership started to do their jobs before it is to late for us. Also the leadership of the UAW needs to keep the pressure on instead of falling back to opportunism for the few to get lazy and fat at the memberships expense.

About the Author

Richard L Hill

Born and raised in the vibrant city of Saginaw, Michigan, I have always been a person who embraces life's challenges and opportunities. Growing up in a tough middle-class neighborhood taught me the importance of hard work, determination, and community spirit. My friends would describe me as a dedicated individual who never misses work without good reason and someone who constantly strives for self-improvement. Throughout my life, I have pursued various passions and interests that have shaped my character and values. As a downhill skier since eighth grade, I took second place in a race at Apple Mountain during my tenth-grade year. This passion eventually led me to join the Michigan National Ski Patrol, where I worked at both Apple Mountain and Boyne Mountain after passing my senior training. These experiences instilled in me the value of perseverance and pushing one's limits. My greatest accomplishments include completing my Bachelor of Business Administration degree from Northwood University, which took 25 years of dedication and persistence. Additionally, I am incredibly proud of my two beautiful daughters who are now happily married, embodying the family values and strong work ethic that I hold dear. Some of the most important values I live by include believing in Jesus, upholding the Constitution of the United States, and advocating for freedom of speech and the right to choose one's career path. I firmly believe that everyone should strive to be the best or one of the best in their chosen vocation and contribute positively to society. Life is a journey, and it is essential to understand that our choices shape our paths. Patience, preparation, and resilience in the face of failure are crucial elements of personal growth. It is vital to find solutions to problems and recognize that not everyone excels in all aspects of life – discovering your unique talents and strengths is key. In my free time, I enjoy snow skiing, golfing, bowling, gaming, learning new things, and spending quality time with family and friends. These hobbies allow me to unwind, recharge, and maintain a healthy work-life balance. If I could time travel to the future and impart wisdom to future generations about living life, I would emphasize the importance of protecting our environment, keeping our oceans clean, and managing the world's resources responsibly. Freedom may not be free, but we must learn to live in harmony with one another and collaborate to explore new worlds. As an individual who has faced numerous challenges and triumphs throughout my life, I am proud of the person I have become today. My experiences have shaped my values, passions, and outlook on life, making me a stronger, more resilient individual. Through hard work, determination, and a never-give-up attitude, I continue to grow, learn, and share my journey with others, inspiring them to embrace their own unique paths in life.

Causes I believe in

I believe in a Union and the Ideology for a class of people working together to perform an honest day's work for an honest day's pay. The union organizes the jobs so that you have the right person which knows the job and how to do it. The right to bargain for a living wage and a comfortable retirement. You also have the right to negotiate for health care coverage. The rest at this stage of the game I give it to the Lord my god.

www.ingramcontent.com/pod-product-compliance
Lightning Source LLC
Chambersburg PA
CBHW051856250726
48659CB00006B/2249